CW00923193

Copyright Notice

Strolling Around Lucca by Irene Reid

ISBN: 9781519044273

Arriving in Lucca

Over the wall

If you arrive by train and have no luggage, the cheapest and most fun way into town is to go over the wall.

Leave the train station and cross the square in front of it. Carefully cross the main road and you will reach the huge green lawn which circles the wall. You will find a path, probably being well used by tourists, which leads you straight to the wall and then turns right. It takes you to an easily negotiated staircase which you should climb, cross the wall, and then take the path on your left to go down on the other side. From there you can navigate to the start of one of the walks.

Through the gate

If you have luggage and your hotel is in the old town and near the station you might prefer to just walk through the gate. If so carefully cross the main road and turn left to reach the Porto San Pietro where you enter Lucca. From there you can navigate to your hotel.

Taxi

Finally if your hotel is right across the other side of Lucca, you might want to use a taxi. You can find a rank outside the station.

Church Times

You will discover that a lot of Lucca's churches shut at midday for a very long lunch. If you suddenly find yourself outside a locked door, it might be a good idea to have a long lunch break yourself, or perhaps hire a bike and tackle Walk 3 Around the Wall.

A Potted History

Lucca started as a small settlement which was swept up by the mighty Roman Empire about 200 BC. Rome extended the little town, and as you explore you will see that even today the roads still follow the typical Roman grid-layout. For defence the Romans surrounded Lucca with its first wall. That wall no longer exists but you can still see traces of the original Roman town in the very heart of the old city

Of course as we all know, the Roman Empire fell when the barbarians invaded from the North. Lucca lay in the path of the Lombards, a tribe who originated in Germany and who eventually became very famous for their banking skills. The locals learned quickly from the invaders and Lucca was soon a prosperous banking centre. In fact it was so successful that it became the capital of the Lombard region of Tuscia.

The Lombards were defeated in the tenth century leaving Lucca to fend for itself. It became an independent city state and moved into the very lucrative silk industry in the eleventh century, producing the most sought after silk in Europe. Lucca soon became even wealthier and the town expanded and blossomed.

How did they manage that? Well Lucca had a sizable Jewish and Greek community who maintained commercial and family links with the countries of the Middle East – which gave them access to a raw silk source. They then had to get the silk into Lucca and Lucca is not near the sea, so Lucca made a deal with the city of Genoa, who agreed to let Lucca's goods flow through their territory and their port. In return Genoa got the business of transporting Lucca's raw silk to and from the Middle East. A good deal for both cities

Lucca also paid their skilled workers very well, which tempted more silk weavers into town. By the fourteenth century business was booming and the thousands of silk looms were pushing out the most beautiful silks, some even woven with gold and silk thread, which they sent to the best cloth markets in Europe, like Bruges and Paris. Nothing lasts forever however, and other Italian cites joined in the trade as time went on, lessening the importance of silk to Lucca.

The second ring of walls went up in the twelfth century extending the city, but they didn't help in 1314 when Lucca's neighbour Pisa invaded. Lucca suffered two years of Pisan rule before throwing the invaders out and handing the reins of power to their war-leader Castruccio Antelminelli. He was incredibly successful, gained power and territory for Lucca, and even held the mighty Florentine army at bay. But after his death Lucca's governors were only interested in personal gain and not Lucca's best interests. This led to multiple revolts and revolutions over the next couple of centuries.

In the fourteenth and fifteenth century the third wall went up, again extending the city outwards. The walls were modified and improved over the centuries to the ones you see today. They have never had to withstand any military action.

Napoleon invaded this part of Italy. He installed his sister, Elisa, as the ruler of Lucca in 1805 and she was a popular and successful leader. When Napoleon finally met his Waterloo, Lucca fell under Spanish rule in the person of Maria Luisa who became the Duchess of Lucca. She was absolutely determined to outdo her predecessor Elisa Bonaparte, and was responsible for the vital aqueduct construction which brought clean fresh water into Lucca from the Pisan hills in the south.

Lucca returned to Tuscany in 1847, but as part of Tuscany it never achieved quite the same importance as it did as an independent state.

The Maps

There are maps sprinkled all through the walks to help you find your way. If you need to check where you are at any point during a walk, always flip back to find the map you need.

The Stars

There are not really many famous people from Lucca, but there are two you will come across as you explore.

Puccini

The first is Puccini, the very famous and successful composer. You will have a chance to visit his home and even hear his wonderful music in his home-town.

Matteo Civitali

The second is Matteo Civitali who is much less well known, but much loved by Lucca. He was a sculptor, architect, and painter, and you will come across a lot of his work as you explore.

Walk 1 – Lucca East

The walk starts in little Piazza del Giglio.

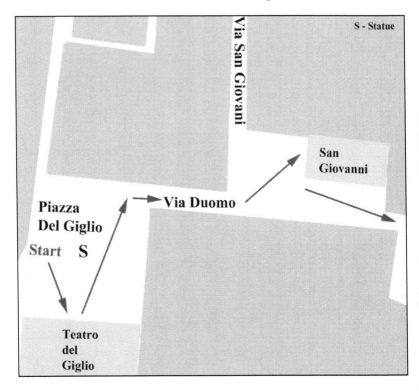

Piazza del Giglio

This little square is an offshoot of the much larger neighbouring Piazza Napoleone. The marble statue in the centre of the square is General Garibaldi.

Garibaldi

He was the soldier who helped to liberate the Italian territories and cities which were ruled by Austria and France in the nineteenth century, and to forge a united Italy in their place. The statue shows him stepping onto Roman soil as part of that liberation.

As a young man he sailed into Russia to trade. He met and was influenced by another young Italian who was a member of Young Italy, a secret organisation fighting for Italian unification. That meeting was a pivotal point in Garibaldi's life as he swore to liberate Italy.

His life was a series of battles and exiles. During his first exile he made his home in Uruguay where he adopted the traditional gaucho red shirt and poncho. This statue has him wearing a poncho.

When he returned to Italy to join the battle for independence, his followers were known as the Red Shirts because they followed their leader and dressed the same way.

Italy went through many battles for independence and the Red Shirts were always involved. Garibaldi managed to liberate Sicily, then Naples, then the entire south of the peninsula. He handed all the lands he had liberated to the King of Sardinia, Victor Emmanuel II, who completed the liberation of Italy to become its first King.

At the base of the pedestal you can see some bronze reliefs showing key scenes in Garibaldi's life. One shows him landing in Sicily, again wearing his poncho. The other shows the Battle of Calatafimi which Garibalidi won as part of his liberation of Sicily.

You will be hard pressed to find a city in Italy which doesn't have a memorial to Garibaldi of some sort. He is even honoured in Great Britain; we named a biscuit after him.

Teatro del Giglio

If you stand face to face with Garibaldi and then turn right, you will see the handsome Teatro del Giglio which the square gets its name from.

It is one of the oldest theatres in Italy, dating from the early sixteenth century. It caught fire in the seventeenth century but was rebuilt and has been in almost constant use ever since.

It was redesigned in the nineteenth century and was named Teatro del Giglio. Right at the top of the theatre you can see Lucca's coat of arms and beneath that:

Teatro Comunale del Giglio

Giglio means lily, and the theatre got that pretty name because three golden lilies appear in the family coat of arms of Maria Luisa, the Duchess of Lucca who ruled at the time.

A low point arrived with WWI when it was turned into a military depot and then abandoned. The good news is that it was carefully restored and is now a working theatre again, popular and much loved by the locals.

This is a nice square to visit in the evening and perhaps have something to eat. If you do, you might see the theatre filling up with eager theatre goers.

Face away from the theatre and walk to the other end of the square. Turn right into Via Duomo to leave Piazza del Giglio and enter another square which holds a church.

Chiesa e Battistero dei SS Giovanni e Reparata

This beautiful old church is now deconsecrated but was once Lucca's cathedral.

Before you go inside take a good look above the main doorway. You can see two lions guarding each side of the door, one fighting yet another lion and the other fighting a dragon - the dragon looks more like a large lizard. Beneath the lions are two cowering figures, watching the battle above them. Between the lions and just above the door runs a wonderful line of angels and saints – all wearing flowing robes. They flank The Virgin Mary who stands with both hands held up.

There is an entrance fee to get in. The best tactic is to buy the combined ticket offered by the church which covers four "sights". It lets you explore this church, its tower, the Cathedral, and the Cathedral Museum.

The church is where Puccini was baptised, and it hosts a concert of his works most evenings of the year, making use of the church's wonderful acoustics. It's nice to absorb some Puccini in his home town, so if that appeals get some tickets whilst you are here.

Go inside. The church has a beautiful golden roof, and beneath it stands two lines of mighty Roman columns. Take a look at the impressive dome, it was studied by architect

Brunelleschi as he puzzled how to build Florence's enormous cathedral dome.

To the left of the altar you can descend to explore an archaeological dig, which lets you see five excavation levels going all the way back to the Romans. You can follow the map you were given at the desk, and if you are really keen you could also hire an audio guide which will give you a lot more detail. However that may be a little dry for most visitors.

You might prefer just to wander along the iron walkways between the various piles of rock and brick, keeping your eyes peeled for the occasional piece of Roman mosaic on the floor – but you won't see anything really extensive. A large colourful portion of Roman pavement was discovered, but sadly it was removed and placed in Lucca's National Museum of Villa Guinigi – it would have been far more interesting if they had left it where they had found it.

Climb back up to ground level and if you have the energy you can climb up the church tower. The door to the tower is on your right, just before the altar. The climb is mostly quite manageable, but the very last section is a small ladder which does require two free hands to negotiate safely. Once at the top you will get great views of Lucca and beyond. Unfortunately the church decided to put a safety mesh around the top in case someone decides to jump, but someone has kindly cut out a couple of holes in it, so at least you can take some good snaps of the view.

Once back down on terra firma, exit the church and turn left to continue along its side.

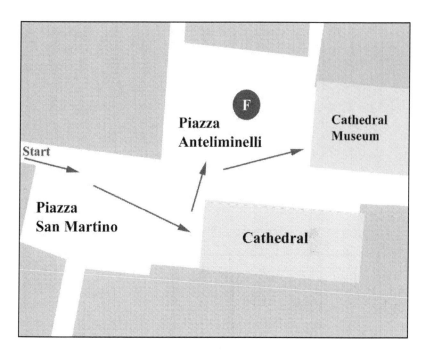

You will reach another larger square in front of the cathedral.

Cattedrale di San Martino

Lucca like most Tuscan towns has a beautiful cathedral.

This one has three ornate archways giving access to three doorways. The third archway is smaller than the other two because the bell tower was already standing when the archways were added, so the final archway had to be squeezed in.

Lucca was an important stop on the Via Francigena which was used by pilgrims to reach Rome from France. The pilgrims of course visited the Cathedral to see its treasures, but it's said that they also stopped under these archways to trade with the money changers.

Stand at the front and take a minute to look up at the ornate columns and their embellishments, each is intricately sculpted. Above the columns are inlays showing us zodiacal symbols, animals, and even some hunting scenes on the upper levels.

There is a legend on just why all the columns of the façade are so different and are even in different colours. When it came to decorating the cathedral Lucca announced a contest for the best column design. Artists came from far and wide, each bringing a column sample to win the competition. However Lucca kept them all, didn't pay the contestants, and used them all on the Cathedral.

Look at the left-hand pilaster at the front of the Cathedral indicated above. It is also intricately carved and it shows the family tree of the Virgin Mary, with Adam and Eve at the bottom and Jesus at the top.

Have a good look at the large carving over the right hand arch. It depicts the story of "St Martin and the beggar". There are many miracles about Saint Martin. This statue shows him giving half his cloak to a passing beggar. Saint Martin had a dream the same night that Jesus was wearing his cloak, and next morning he discovered that his cloak had miraculously regrown its missing half. The sculpture you see is a copy, as the original is deemed far too precious to be left outside and is inside for safe keeping.

The smaller carvings above the doors are by Nicola Pisano, a very famous sculptor from Pisa. There is also a line of workers above one of the doors, each little figure depicting a month and what task had to be tackled in that month. For instance September was the threshing month. They are all a bit worn now and perhaps in need of restoration

Now stand back from the church and look at the beautiful bell tower on your right - it seems to get lighter and more graceful as it rises – an effect of the number of windows which increases on the upper levels, making it appear more open. The tower is not open to the public so you are saved another climb.

Find the mysterious labyrinth engraved into the right hand side of the smallest archway. No-one knows why it is there although some believe it was a sign that the faithful must follow God to find their way.

The Latin inscription at its side refers to the Greek legend of Theseus, who entered the Labyrinth to battle the Minotaur. Theseus found his way back out with help of Ariadne's thread which he tied to the entrance before venturing in.

HIC QUEM CRETICUS EDIT. DAEDALUS EST
LABERINTHUS
DE QUO NULLUS VADERE QUIVIT QUI FUIT INTUS
NI THESEUS GRATIS ADRIANE STAMINE JUTUS

Or for anyone whose Latin isn't quite up to it:

This is the labyrinth built by Daedalus of Crete
all who entered therein were lost
save Theseus, thanks to Ariadne's thread

There is a legend that anyone condemned to death in Lucca was brought to the Cathedral. If the condemned was able to trace a path out of the labyrinth on one attempt he would be spared.

Go inside the cathedral to explore. The floor is full of green and white marble squares with geometric designs in the middle. Walk around the church in an anti-clockwise direction.

You will first find the original marble "St Martin and the beggar" statue which was rescued from outside. Walk down the right hand side of the cathedral to find the very colourful Last Supper by Tintoretto. You can spot it easily by the red robes worn by many of the figures. Tintoretto was a pupil of Titian, who was famous for his love of red, and Tintoretto clearly agreed with him.

Ilaria de Carretto

On the right hand side of the altar enter the Sacristy to visit the marble sarcophagus of Ilaria de Carretto, the second wife of Paolo Guinigi who was once Lord of Lucca. They married in 1403 in a very grand wedding but sadly she died in childbirth a few years later. This beautiful sarcophagus was carved by Quercia, a famous sculptor from near Siena. Ilaria's beloved dog is carved at her feet, and a line of little cherubs runs along the side of the sarcophagus.

The Italian poet Gabriele D'Annunzio wrote a poem called *Lucca*, and in it he mentions this beautiful sarcophagus

> And the city from the arched circle,
> Where the Guinigi woman sleeps.

Oddly though, Ilaria's remains are not actually there. This sarcophagus is a monument and it is empty. It's thought her remains have recently been excavated in the church of San Francesco, where the Guinigi family had a chapel.

It seems that Paolo Guinigi didn't have much luck in his brides. His first wife was just a teenager, and she is thought to have died of the plague. He married his third wife in 1420 and she died just two years later. The same excavation which seems to have found Ilaria, also found two other females of the right age in the chapel and they might be Paolo's other two wives.

Paolo Guinigi was lord of Lucca but he became a hated tyrant. Finally Lucca revolted and he was arrested and died in prison. Poor Ilaria's sarcophagus was stripped of its decoration other than what you see now, and it was shuffled from one part of the cathedral to another because the authorities couldn't decide what to do with it. It was not until centuries later that it was restored and placed for everyone to admire. It finally arrived here in the Sacristy only in 1995.

You can also find the Madonna and Child by Ghirlandaio in the sacristy

Madonna and Child by Ghirlandaio

Here Mary and Jesus are surrounded by various saints who seem to be having a rather informal chat with the baby Jesus. On the left is Saint Peter holding his keys, Saint Sebastian holds an arrow, presumably one of many used to kill him, and Saint Paul has his sword. The final visitor is Saint Clement wearing his bishop's mitre. The whole painting is an orange glow.

Volto Santo

Cross the cathedral, passing several sculptures by Matteo Civitali on either side of the altar as you do. He was the local artist mentioned in the Potted History, whose work you will meet again on this walk.

Turn towards the main door and you will reach the Volto Santo in its a ornate temple. The temple is called the Tempietto and was also designed by Civitali.

The Volto Santo itself is carved from a cedar of Lebanon, a tree which was often used for very sacred items in biblical times. These beautiful trees were almost wiped out by deforestation especially in The Lebanon. The cedar is choosy in its environment, preferring to grow in good deep soil at high altitudes with lots of rain and light – it once covered Mount Lebanon but now only survives in small patches. However Turkey has recently come to the rescue and now plants more and more cedars every year.

Legend tells us that the Volto Santo was carved by Nicodemus who was present at the Crucifixion. The hand of God took over and carved the face. It was then carried on a crewless ship to Luni, a port in Tuscany, before arriving in Lucca on a driverless cart. The Volo Santo was placed in the church of Saint Frediano. Next morning it had disappeared, and after a huge search it was found in the garden of Saint Martin. This was interpreted as a broad hint by God and the crucifix was moved into Saint Martin permanently.

It's a nice tale but the crucifix is actually from about the 13th century. However the facts don't stop the faithful walking around Lucca in a torch-lit procession called the Luminaria di Santa Croce, which celebrates its arrival in Lucca. The crucifix used to be carried in the procession, garbed in a bejeweled robe. However it's now deemed too precious and delicate, so the robe goes on its own, and the crucifix stays safely in the cathedral. The procession walks from San Frediano to Saint Martin in September – recreating the journey of the crucifix when it disappeared. It's a major event in the calendar, and is so well attended that the procession is already entering Saint Martin before it has completely emptied from San Frediano.

There are many legends about the Volto Santo, one of the best is the story of the silver slipper. A poor minstrel arrived in Lucca and wanted to give something precious to the Volto Santo, but of course he had nothing. So he gave the only gift he had, he played his lute beautifully. Jesus rewarded the musician by dropping one of his silver slippers for him to pick up – which the minstrel did. The authorities took a very dim view of the miracle, arrested him for theft and he was condemned to death. The minstrel prayed desperately for help and Jesus sent an angel to intercede and corroborate his story. The minstrel was freed and the angel disappeared.

The Volto Santo appears in Dante's Divine Comedy. In his depiction of the fifth pit of hell, Dante immerses the sinners in boiling pitch and has them tortured by devils. Dante was famous for populating his stories with people he did not like. One of the sinners in the fifth pit is Martin Bottario, who came from Lucca, and who Dante thought had once overcharged him. The devils tell Bottario not to bother praying to the

Volto Santo of Lucca, because he is in eternal damnation. Scary stuff!

Before you move on, make sure you look behind the Tempietto to find the statue of San Sebastian – also by Civitali.

Leave the cathedral and the square on your right is Piazza Antelminelli.

Piazza Antelminelli

This square was named after the family whose palace was demolished to build the square. The Antelminelli family members were key figures in Lucca's history, and you will meet them again on this walk. In fact the first teenage bride of Paolo Guinigi, who you have just been reading about in the cathedral, was Maria Caterina Antelminelli.

The square has a fountain sporting lion heads pouring water into the basin, surrounded by small marble columns which are chained together. The marble is from Carrara, Michelangelo's favourite quarry.

The fountain was originally supplied by the aqueduct built in the nineteenth century which brought precious clean water from the Pisan hills into Lucca. This is a nice spot for a café stop if you need one.

Guelphs and Ghibellines

Most of Tuscany was either in the Guelph or the Ghibelline camp, or to put it simply supported the Pope or the Monarchy. Even within the individual cities the population was split along these lines, which often meant betrayals and revolts as each side lost or gained control for a time. Most of the twelfth through fourteenth centuries were full of battles between the two sides; long after the rest of Europe had moved on to find other things to fight about.

Lucca was no different, the Antelminelli family was Ghibelline and at one time actually ruled Lucca, however they only stayed in power for one generation and were removed by the Guelphs.

Now stand between the fountain and the cathedral and face the side of the cathedral. Turn left and in front of you stand the three buildings which now make up the Cathedral Museum.

Cathedral Museum

This museum contains various religious antiques, but the highlight is the bejeweled garments and the golden crown now carried in place of the Volto Santo during the September parade. They are studded with diamonds and very, very valuable. You will find them on the ground floor in glass cases.

The museum meanders in various directions over several floors and there are some other items worth a look. The museum is modern, its exhibits are well laid out, and it's worth spending a little time looking round.

Upstairs in one of the display cabinets you can find the ivory Consular Diptych of Areobindus - which was carved way back in the sixth century. A consular diptych was a very ornate commemoration of someone getting promoted to

Roman Consul, and this is one of the very few which have survived intact through the centuries.

A Roman consul was at one time a valued leader and advisor of the Roman Republic, but by the time of the Caesars it had become just a title given to favourites of the emperor. Caligula planned to make his horse, Incitatus, a Roman Consul - but was killed before he got round to it. Aerobindus was made Roman Consul after a successful military career, and retired to Constantinople.

There is also a casket from Limoges in France, showing the assassination of the priest Thomas Becket. King Henry II of England wanted him dispatched because Becket vehemently fought against the King's actions. Becket finally excommunicated the King and paid the ultimate price. Henry is quoted as saying "Who will rid me of this troublesome priest" and this casket shows some golden knights fulfilling his request by stabbing Becket.

On the first floor you can also reach a balcony which gives you a viewpoint over the entire square.

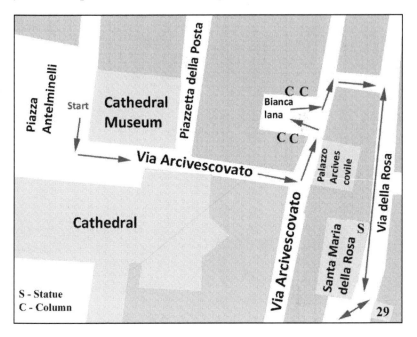

With the museum main door behind you turn left then left again, to walk alongside the wall of the Cathedral on Via Arcivescovato. You will reach a piazza on your right. If you come in spring it will boast some nice green lawns which turn brown as the heat of summer parches them.

Palazzo Arcivescovile

Walk straight ahead along the edge of the lawn to reach number 45 Via Arcivescovato, the Palazzo Arcivescovile where the Archbishop resides – it has a lovely old door adorned with a pair of cherubs.

It also houses Lucca's extraordinary archive - a priceless collection of documents covering Lucca's history from before the time of the Lombards. It holds about 13,000 scrolls some going back as far as 685 AD! It is a uniquely complete collection of both religious and civic documents – providing a treasure trove to students of Lucca's history.

Turn left to walk along Via Arcivescovato. After just a few steps you will reach a little in-shot on your left called Corte Biancalana.

Corte Biancalana

This little court was named after the Biancalana family who came to Lucca in 1540. It used to be the cloister of an old graveyard, and you can see that the cloister columns have been built into the surrounding walls.

Continue along Via Arcivescovato and after just a few more steps turn right, still on Via Arcivescovato. Turn right again into Via della Rosa and walk down a block to find the old church of Santa Maria Della Rosa on your right.

Santa Maria della Rosa

This little church is interesting for a few reasons.

You might wonder at the name of the church. In Roman times the area just outside the town wall was used for grazing sheep. Legend says that a shepherd, who was dumb from birth, noticed his sheep avoiding a nice juicy green bush. Curiosity made him look and he discovered a beautiful rose, which was a bit of a surprise as it was January. He picked the rose to show his father and suddenly he could speak. A miracle!

The bishop was informed of the miracle, and he revealed that long ago there had been an image of the Virgin holding three roses where the rose bush grew. So a little oratory was created there which later became this church.

Have a look at the statue of the Virgin holding roses in her hand on the corner of the church. Some art historians believe the statue was carved by Pisano – you saw more of his work in the Cathedral.

Below the statue is a very ancient plaque which translates as:

In honour of God and of the Blessed Virgin Mary of the Rose
this work was done at the time of Bianco di Bifolco,
Luporo Viviani, Nuccoro speziale, operari, in 1309

There are more beautifully carved roses running up the side of a door near the statue. A little further on is the main door which is also decorated with roses, as are the windows.

Walk round to the back of the church and if the little door is open, go inside. You will find one of the few remaining sections of the original Roman wall built into the fabric of the church – it's on the left-hand side as you enter.

There is a fourteenth century painting of the Madonna Della Rosa on the altar. It's considered to be one of the most important paintings in Lucca. It was moved from the back of the church to its current position in the seventeenth century and was badly damaged – losing two saints in the process.

This is also the church where Gemma Galgani worshipped; she is one of Lucca's saints. She is actually quite a modern saint as she only died in 1903 at the age of 25. She apparently had many visions of Jesus and the Virgin Mary, suffered stigmata, and levitated. She is the patron saint of students although I doubt many have heard of her. Just to the right of the door as you enter is the bench she prayed at, and it is often decked in flowers from pilgrims.

When you exit the church you will find Gemma's picture above the door of number 29 – where she died of tuberculosis.

Return the way you came to return to the junction with Via Arcivescovato.

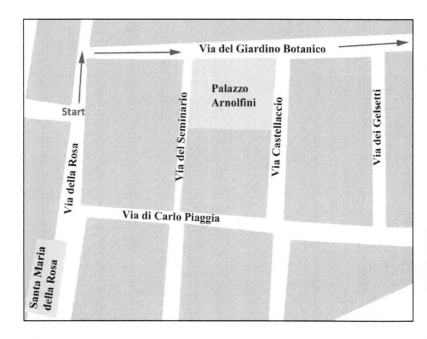

Continue straight ahead along Via Della Rosa but then take the next right into Via Della Giardino Botanico, a partly tree-lined road. Pass Via del Seminario on your right and to reach the front of the Palazzo Arnolfni.

Palazzo Arnolfini

It was built by the Arnolfini family who made their fortune in the silk industry and banking in the sixteenth century. You might recognise the name Arnolfini, because one of The London National Gallery's most famous paintings is the Arnolfini Portrait by Van Eyck. The family had moved to Bruges in Belgium by the time that was painted.

The palace was sold to the church and over the next few centuries it was used as an orphanage and a home for illegal immigrants. Things took a turn for the better in 1990 when it was sold again, and this time the owners turned it into luxury apartments with a beautiful garden in the courtyard.

Continue along Via Della Giardino Botanico passing Via Castellaccio and Via dei Gelesetti on your right.

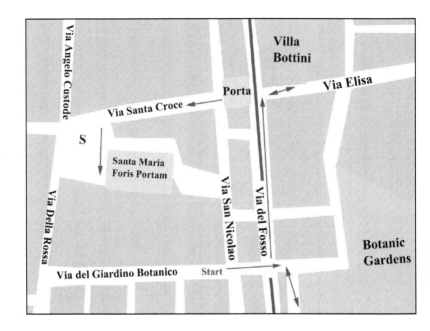

Cross Via San Nicolao and a canal, beyond which you turn right up a ramp - it leads up to the city wall. However the Botanic Garden is through a wrought iron gate on your left – there is an entrance fee.

Giardino Botanico

You will be given a little map to find your way around, although the garden is not very large so you will not get lost!

At the bottom of the entrance steps you will see a rather uninviting tunnel on the right. Do go in, as it will take you under the wall which is quite fun. When you reach the main corridor turn right to reach the cannon ball garden which makes a nice snap. Make your way back to the garden.

The garden was founded by the Duchesse of Lucca for education and research, and hosts many rare and exotic trees and plants. The oldest tree is a cedar of Lebanon planted in 1820. If you are lucky enough to be there in the right season you will see the Magnolia Grandiflora covered in beautiful globes of white, or perhaps the rhododendrons covered in bright blooms.

You will eventually reach the little pond which is fed by an ancient spring and which boasts a legend. Sit down, gaze into the water, and rest your feet.

You might see Lucida Mansi. Lucida Mansi was a beautiful woman who led a wild and expensive lifestyle in the seventeenth century. She had many, many lovers. She was very vain and surrounded herself with mirrors so she could always see her reflection. When the ravages of time started to touch her she couldn't take it, so she struck a deal with the devil - she got another thirty years of beauty for her soul. Time ran out eventually and the devil appeared to claim his prize - he dragged Lucida round the walls of Lucca in a fiery carriage, which then plunged into the little pond you see before you to reach hell. On stormy nights that fiery carriage is said to career around the wall always ending up in the pond. Also it's said that Lucida's face can be seen gazing up from the depths.

Less romantically, history tells us she died of the plague and is buried in the family vault.

When you leave the garden, walk straight down the ramp and into Via del Fosso.

Via del Fosso

This is a lovely old street with a canal running down the centre. It was originally the moat outside the town wall – you will see a bit of that town wall soon. Not too far down the road you will find a fountain just next to a grand archway. Apparently the head the water gushes from is Bacchus, the Roman God of Wine.

Turn right into Via Elisa to reach Villa Bottini on the left.

Villa Bottini

This is one of the few gardens in Lucca you can take a walk around. The villa was owned by a wealthy family in the sixteenth century, but by the twentieth century it was abandoned and was very much in need of repair. Lucca bought it and it's now sometimes used for exhibitions, but it is rather tired looking and needs someone to renovate it to its former glory.

Walk around the villa to reach the garden, which also needs some care, but you can imagine how beautiful it could be. It has a fountain, an archway, and a grotto – all in disrepair.

Leave the garden by the gate you entered, and turn right to return to Via del Fosso. Now you can admire Porta San Gervasio which rears up ahead of you.

Porta San Gervasio

The Porta is one of the gateways through the old town wall and was built in 1255. The old town wall was more or less demolished and replaced with the current wall, leaving just this gateway and another gateway you will visit later.

It's thought that there was once a walkway at the top running between the two towers. These days the towers are private dwellings.

Go through the archway but look back once you are through – the inner archway is decorated with lovely golden stars and some elderly frescoes which were discovered during the restoration, and carefully restored as much as possible.

Walk along Via Santa Croce, one of Lucca's main streets, to reach a square, Piazza Santa Maria Foris Portam.

Colonna Mozza

You can see the Colonna Mozza (broken column) in the square. It is believed that it was used as the finishing post of a horse race in medieval times. The horses entering the race had to be unshod, and they raced around the streets of Lucca to reach this column. It was a famous race and horses were entered from all over Tuscany. Even "Lorenzo the Magnificent", a member of the all-powerful Medici family from Florence sent a horse to win the prize.

On your left is the church of Santa Maria Foris Portam.

Santa Maria Foris Portam

This church was built in white limestone and is called Santa Maria Bianca by the locals because of its colour. The name Foris Portam is Latin and tells us that the church was originally outside the medieval wall, which is now long gone. The church was extended upwards in the sixteenth century but you can see that the brickwork was never faced.

There are three doors at the front. Take a look above the left hand door and you will see an interesting byzantine-style depiction of the Virgin Mary, quite different from the normal European style.

The church is not open very often, but if you do get a chance pop in.

The Altar

The altar is the work of Civitali, one of Tuscany's most famous sculptors whose work you have already seen in other churches.

Santa Lucia – Guercino

You can see a painting of Santa Lucia. She gouged out her own eyes and is portrayed as presenting them to heaven on a plate – however the artist clearly couldn't bring himself to portray her as she would have appeared, as she still has her eyes in place.

There is evidence of Lucca's Roman past here. Find the Roman sarcophagus which has been turned into a font – it sits in an in-shot of the wall and has colourful frescoes above it.

There is also a camera obscura inside. Spot the line running across the church floor. The sun shines through a hole in the right hand wall and when it touches the line, it means it is noon in Lucca. There is a plaque telling you that it is exactly seven minutes and fifty-five seconds behind Rome.

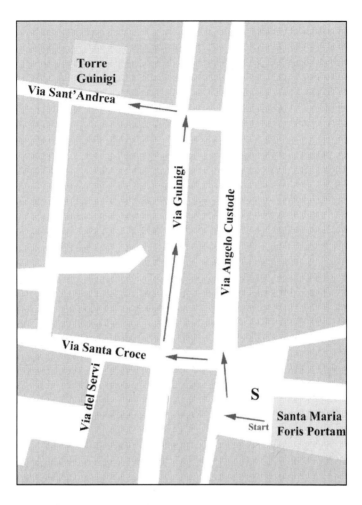

Leave the church and cross the square diagonally right. Continue along Via Santa Croce and then take the second on the right, Via Guinigi. This road is named after the very powerful Guinigi family – the family which Ilaria became part of when she married Paoli Guinigi. It is lined by old medieval palaces - walk along it to reach a junction with Via Sant'Andrea on the left. Turn left and on your right you will find the Torre Guinigi.

Torre Guinigi

Of course you must climb this tower, both for the view and to see the trees which crown it. But you will return this way later on in the walk, so you could leave the climb until then if it's a bit too soon after the previous tower.

This tower was built by the Guinigi family at a time when any family with the wealth and power built a tower to show off and to hide in when attacked. The Guinigi family's last member bequeathed the tower to Lucca in his will.

It's thought the roof-garden with its holm oak trees was installed in the fifteenth century, although the trees have been replanted since then. The trees represent rebirth, so it's a bit sad that the family actually died out.

There is a legend of course. It's said that the tallest tree was planted by Paolo Guinigi. During Lucca's turbulent history he was captured and imprisoned by the Duke of Milan and he later died in prison. It's said that at the moment of his capture all the leaves fell off the tree.

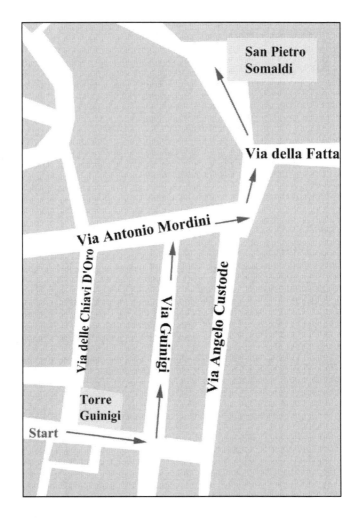

When you have had enough of gazing at the rooftops, leave the tower. Turn left to return to the junction with Via Guinigi. Turn left into Via Guinigi and follow it to the T junction with Via Antonio Mordini.

Turn right and follow Via Antonio Mordini as it bends left. Pass Via della Fatta on your right and enter a square called Piazza San Pietro Somaldi.

Carlo del Prete

As you do, you will see a plaque on your left on Palazzo Del Prete. It's dedicated to Carlo del Prete who came from Lucca and lived in the palazzo.

He was Italy's greatest aviator who set more than one world record in the 1920's when daring airmen first took to the sky. His most famous record was the "Four Continents" tour when he was part of the small team which flew the Santa Maria flying boat across four continents, Europe, America, Asia, and Africa. They flew over 29,000 miles in 123 days.

His family has tried to preserve his memory – hence the plaque. But Lucca seems oddly uninterested in the achievements of one of its sons.

Walk further into the square and you will see the church of San Pietro Somaldi on your right.

San Pietro Somaldi

Walk over to the church and take a look above the door to see the engraving of Saint Peter being given the Keys to Heaven by Jesus.

Find the "Devils scratch", several furrows on the pillars of the entrance. Urban legend tells us they were put there by the devil. He tried but failed to hurt Gemma Galgani, the modern saint you read about when you visited Santa Maria della Rosa.

If you go in you will see Gemma's photograph on the right-hand wall.

Also look at the much-admired organ which was originally constructed by a famous Lucchese organist called Cacioli.

Puccini played on the organ as a young man and thought very highly of it, so years later when the organ was in need of restoration he recommended Tronci from nearby Pistoia. Tronci had already built several organs used to perform Puccini's operas and Puccini thought highly of him.

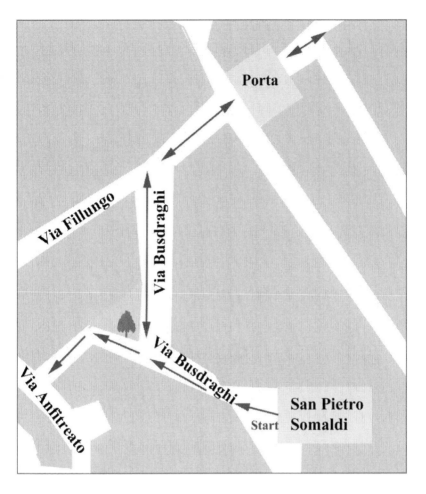

Leave the church and follow the right hand wall into Via Busdraghi. Follow this road to a fork in the road where you can see some trees overhanging a garden wall.

Gate Diversion

As mentioned Lucca's walls were extended three times. If you would like to see another of the gates from the second extension, take a little diversion. It is only a five minute walk there and back.

Take the main right-hand road, still on Via Busdgraghi and at its end turn right onto Via Fillungo.

Lamberti Lando

There is another plaque on your right-hand side at number 188, also celebrating one of Lucca's sons. Lando was a composer of operas but never achieved the fame and success of Puccini. One of his best received works was called "Nelly", inspired by The Old Curiosity Shop by Charles Dickens whose heroine was of course Nell.

Continue along Via Fillungo.

Porta dei Borghi

As you walk along you will see an enormous archway ahead of you, and beside it is another huge archway which has been filled in. This is one of Lucca's surviving medieval gates, the Porta dei Borghi from the thirteenth century - the gate is decorated by a frieze of the Madonna.

It gives you an idea of the size of the walls at that time. It sits in part of the old wall and is guarded by two side towers, both of which are private dwellings – to see them you should go through the archway to the other side of the gate.

Return by backtracking along Via Fillungo and turn left onto Via Busdraghi to return to the fork in the road.

End of diversion

With Via Busdraghi on your right-hand side, walk along the smaller Via del Portico. It will bend round to the left and bring you onto Via Antitreato.

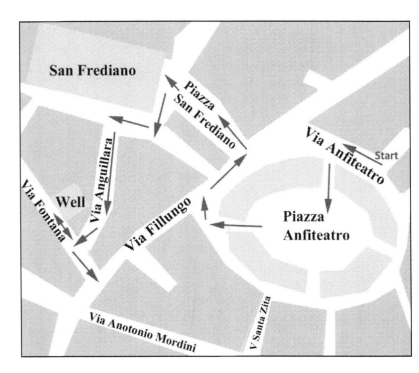

Antitreato

The Anfitreato is built on top of and incorporates the remains of the old Roman amphitheatre which stood here.

Turn right and then take the first entry point on your left through an archway to reach the old Amphitheatre grounds. The square is actually a few feet higher than the original amphitheatre floor.

The Roman amphitheatre which once stood here was built with fifty-four arches and could house ten thousand spectators. They could watch the usual Roman entertainments including of course gladiator games. The amphitheatre was built during the reign of Emperor Claudius.

When the Roman Empire crumbled the population moved in and colonised it – it was much safer inside than outside now that the protection of Rome had gone. They first filled in the archways to give them a defensive wall, and then filled the interior with homes and buildings. It remained that way for centuries. Most of the marble and decorations were lifted and placed in Lucca's churches. By the nineteenth century the centre space was also used as a market. It was not until later in the nineteenth century that Lucca began to remove the added buildings and restore what was left of the original structure to what you see today.

Nowadays there are many cafes and shops here if you need a little rest. It's also nice to visit at night when it's all lit up.

Cross to the middle of the square and you will see that there are four gates into the amphitheatre. One of the gates, the smallest one, is sited exactly on the original Roman entrance.

When you are ready to move on, find the gate which has an inscribed panel above it – it should be the one you entered by. Face it and leave by the archway on your left which will take you onto Via Anfitreato again. Turn right to reach the T junction with Via Fillungo where you turn right once more.

Via Fillungo

This is Lucca's busiest shopping street but has not lost its charm. The Romans built two main roads through Lucca. This part of Via Fillungo follows one of them, the Cardo Maximus, which just meant it was the "main street which runs north to south".

It's just a few steps to reach the second left onto Piazza San Frediano, and to approach the Basilica di San Frediano.

Basilica di San Frediano

San Frediano was an Irish monk who went on a pilgrimage to Rome, but decided to stop and become a hermit in the mountains near Lucca. He was promoted to bishop of Lucca by the Pope.

Lucca was always in danger from the nearby river Serchio, and on one perilous occasion the locals appealed to their bishop to save them. Frediano first prayed and then used a borrowed rake to dig a furrow which he commanded the river to follow. He led the river safely away from Lucca.

He had the San Vincenzo church built on this spot on top of an even older church. He was buried in it and the church was then renamed to San Frediano in his honour. What you see today is a twelfth century face-lift.

Look at the huge gleaming mosaic of the Ascension on the outside before you go in. The Ascension is the moment when Jesus returned to heaven after the resurrection while the twelve disciples watch from below. In this rendition two angels lift the throne of Jesus upwards. The Ascension appears in many works of art, and in this one it's made of gold leaf that glows on a sunny day.

The Virgin Mary used to also be up there – standing in the middle of the disciples. However she suffered the indignity of being replaced by the window you see now.

If you take the cycle trip round the wall on walk 3, you will see how close the church stands to the wall. In fact its lovely bell-tower was used as a defence tower in the middle ages.

Go inside and first admire the columns leading you towards the altar. They are topped with Roman capitals pinched from the old Roman amphitheatre which you have just visited. It feels a very spacious church with its long nave stretching in front of you. Count the columns as you walk along the nave – the fifth on the left and the sixth on the right give you a glimpse of the colourful frescoes which are all that remain of the original frescoes which covered the church.

Fonte Lustrale

On your right is the church's highlight, the sculpted baptismal font, The Fonte Lustrale, from the twelfth century. Have a close look - you can see the story of Moses on the outer panels.

First you can see the desperation of Moses's family when the Pharaoh orders the death of all Jewish boy children. Next Moses's mother gives her child to the Pharaoh's daughter. That's followed by some miracles by Moses, and then the biggest carving, the crossing of the Red Sea. Finally we see the burning bush and the Ten Commandments.

Find the Crossing of the Red Sea where the soldiers of the Egyptian army appear as Medieval Knights in pursuit of the Jews. If you look closely you will see that one of the riders is facing the wrong way round from the waist down. No-one knows why.

Right at the top of the font above red marble pillars, we see a representation of the twelve months of the year. They are mostly represented by some sort of agricultural activity. It's quite difficult to make out exactly who or what each figure is doing, so here is a list:

January - Janus the two faced God
February -a man holding a plant
March - a man taking a thorn out of his foot
April - a man holding a flower
May - a man on horseback
June - a man cutting wheat
July - a man beating wheat
August - a man on horseback
September -a man pressing grapes
October - a man collecting fruit
November -a man ploughing with oxen
December - a man slaughtering a pig

We are actually lucky to be able to see it here in the church. In the eighteenth century it was taken apart and the various pieces were dispersed to other locations. It was only reassembled in the twentieth century, using some old sketches which showed the masons what it originally looked like.

Capella Fatinelli

The Cappella Fatinelli is just behind the Font. It holds the mummified remains of Saint Zita in a glass case. She was a servant of the Fatinelli family, who made their fortune from the silk industry.

Zita was very kind and always wanted to help the poor, so she stole bread from the kitchen she worked in and gave it to the starving. She was caught by her employer one day who demanded to know what was hidden in her apron. Zita claimed it was roses and flowers – you can probably guess the next bit, the bread had transformed into roses and flowers.

According to legend, when Zita died the bells of Lucca's churches spontaneously began to toll. After her death her fame grew as miracles were attributed to her, and she even gets a mention in Dante's Divine Comedy.

All this happened in the thirteenth century. In the sixteenth century she was exhumed and it was found that her body had not decayed – so clearly a very holy person. She was put in a silver casket and she became a saint in the seventeenth century. She is still remarkably well preserved but that is due to mummification.

Saint Zita was very popular across Europe including England. In fact the Knights Hospitaller's church in the village of Eagle in Lincolnshire claims to have her little toe and a lock of her hair! Eagle itself became a place of pilgrimage and the saint is known there as Saint Sithe. The authorities at San Frediano have not admitted to the loss of a toe.

Lucca celebrates their beloved saint on April 27th, when they take her out of the church to a festival of flowers outside the church door

Blood of Christ

When the Volto Santo arrived in Lucca, it was accompanied by a phial of Christ's blood which has always remained in this church. Find the Chapel of the Holy Blood where two angels guard the door to the phial.

Trenta chapel

This beautiful chapel is on the right-hand side of the high altar.

This is where Richard the Pilgrim is buried. He was once a King of Wessex, an ancient kingdom in southwestern England, but he gave it all up to travel on a pilgrimage to Rome with his two sons. He got as far as Lucca where he caught a fever and died, then miracles started happening near his tomb and he became a saint.

Saint Richard is still revered by the people of Lucca - they call him King of the English which is a bit of an exaggeration. This shrine was commissioned by Lorenzo Trento, a wealthy merchant who was clearly a fan of Richard. He and his wife are entombed in front of the altar. The beautifully carved shrine was carved by master sculptor Quercia, and Saint Richard is under the altar.

Chapel of the Cross

Also worth finding is the Chapel of the Cross, full of very colourful frescoes on a vivid blue background. Most interesting is the right-hand side where the fresco depicts Saint Frediano diverting the river Serchio away from Lucca.

On the other wall you can see Bishop Giovanni arranging the transport of the Volto Santo from Luni to Lucca on a driverless cart. Luni was an ancient port in Tuscany where the ship carrying the Volto Santo landed. Luni was destroyed by various invaders in the tenth century and now only exists as an archaeological dig.

One more statue worth finding is another Civitali, the Madonna of the Annunciation where Mary is wearing a purple dress and looks surprised on hearing the news of her unexpected pregnancy.

When you exit the church, turn right to walk around the church corner - you will get a good view of the church tower.

San Frediano Tower

The darker stone at the bottom was the original tower from before the twelfth century. The top of the tower was rebuilt in white stone in the thirteenth century. It still has six bells which were rung in the traditional way until the mid-nineteenth century when electricity took over the job of moving the clappers.

Turn left into Via Anguillar to be greeted by a bust of Pompeo Batoni on the first house on the left where he was born. He was a very successful artist from the eighteenth century who clearly wanted to be remembered, as he gave this bust of himself to Lucca. His works are in many of the main galleries of Europe.

Walk down Via Anguillar and you will reach a T junction with Via Fontana. Take a short diversion by turning right into Via Fontana and a few steps will take you to the Well of Santa Zita on your right.

Well of Santa Zita

This is where the city's favourite saint came to fetch water. The well shaft is now a shrine and you can see the engraving of Santa Zita giving water to the poor.

Backtrack along Via Fontana past Via Anguillara on your left and you will reach the junction with Via Fillungo.

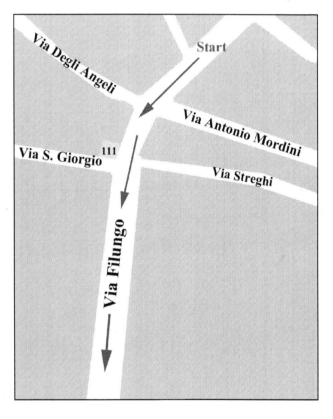

Turn right to walk down Via Fillungo. Pause at Via Antonio Mordini on your left and notice that the street actually has two names. Its officially sanctioned name is Via Antonio

Mordini, named after a politician from the nineteenth century. But the locals prefer to stick to its old name, Via Nouva, even though the street is actually very old.

Continue along Via Fillungo and enjoy looking in the shops as you do.

Pellegrini

At number 111 on your right you will see one of Lucca's lovely Art Nouveau shop facades. This one is a jewellers called Pellegrini and it has the typical golden lettering and a stone sculpture. The Art Nouveau façade was added at the start of the twentieth century.

Go straight on at the next crossroads.

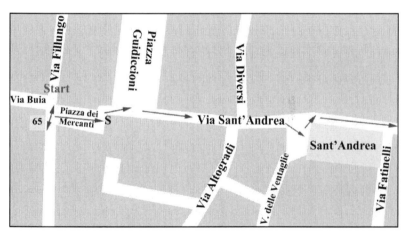

Eventually you will reach the crossroads with Piazza dei Mercanti and Via Buia. Have a glance along Via Buia on your right. It means Dark Street, and it gets that name because the tall buildings along it stop the sunshine reaching the ground.

Take a few steps further into Via Fillungo to have a look at the lovely shop at number 65. It was built as a perfume shop and it has a beautiful Art Nouveau façade with some very pretty ladies dancing in veils. It apparently caused outrage when it was first constructed in 1922, as Lucca was very conservative.

Now turn left into little Piazza dei Mercanti – there is beautiful statue of Mary and the baby Jesus on the corner of the building at the far end of the square.

Leave the square by Via Sant'Andrea passing Piazza Guidiccioni and Via Diversi on your left. A little further on your right you will reach another tiny square with a church – this is Sant'Andrea which the road gets its name from

Sant'Andrea

You can see that like several other churches in Lucca, the door is guarded with two lions. This time they are fighting two warriors and the warriors are definitely getting the worst of it.

Continue along Via Sant'Andrea passing Via Fatinelli on your right.

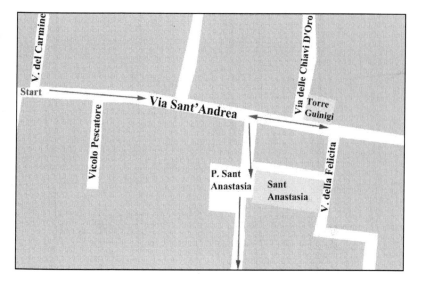

As you walk along you will spot Torre Guinigi with its trees at the top. Walk to the Tower door. If you didn't climb it earlier, you could tackle it now.

When you are ready to move on, stand at the tower door facing the street and turn right. Take the first street on your left, narrow Via Sant'Anastasio. It quickly widens and you will find another old church on your left, Sant'Anastasio.

Sant'Anastasio

The first church on this spot was built in 844, but this one is much more recent from the thirteenth century. The white limestone façade has two wonderful lions guarding the door. Just beside the right-hand lion is a man's head, and the left-hand lion is accompanied by a bull.

Continue walking down Via Sant'Anastasio.

You will pass the Musical Institute (Biblioteca Istituto Musicale Luigi Boccherini) on your right - you might hear students practicing. You will also pass Santa Giulia on your left as you make your way to the adjoining square, Piazza del Suffragio

Santa Giulia

The first church known to have been built on this site was put up in the tenth century, but the experts have found even older tombs which date back to when the Lombards ruled Lucca.

The current church is still very old, coming from the thirteenth century. Look at the decoration around the arches on the front and you will see some female heads with strangely elongated necks.

Leave the church behind, and in the little square in front of the door is a statue of Luigi Boccherini, another of Lucca's musical sons. He was a cellist and we see him playing his instrument. Behind Luigi is the Biblioteca Istituto Musicale Luigi Boccherini, which is the Archive of sheet music and named after him.

Stand face to face with Luigi and turn left. The first building on your right is the Chiesa del Suffragio.

Chiesa del Suffragio

It is now deconsecrated and is used as an auditorium for the musical institute next door. It was built on top of the burial ground for plague victims – hence the name.

Once past the church take the first street on your left, Via del Suffragio.

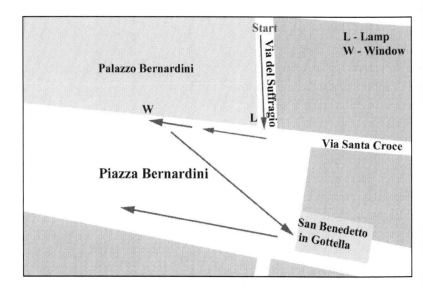

Walk into Piazza Bernardini.   On your right is Palazzo Bernardini.

Palazzo Bernardini

Look up to spot the lovely old lamp holder on the corner of the palace.

The Bernardini's were a very powerful family in the sixteenth century.   Martino Bernardini was the governor in 1545 and he devised the Martinian law in 1556.   It more or less made it impossible for anyone who wasn't from Lucca to hold public office in Lucca.   Over time the law became even more restrictive, so that by 1787 only members of the top eighty families in Lucca could govern.   That came to an end when Napoleon invaded.

Look to the right of the main door to find the Devil's Stone. It is part of the first window on the ground floor and you will see that it curves very oddly. Of course there is a legend.

The Bernardini family built their palace on top of a holy site where the Virgin Mary had once appeared. They also destroyed the statue of the Madonna which stood there. In retribution, their palace developed this kink in its stonework. The workmen building the palace apparently replaced the stone three times with a straight stone, but each time it became warped. It does look like someone has pushed it out from the inside.

Stand with the palazzo behind you and cross the square diagonally left to reach a church.

Chiesa di San Benedetto in Gottella

The little church on the square is another of Lucca's ancient places of worship, first built in the tenth century and more or less rebuilt in the thirteenth century. Just to the right of the door is a sign which identifies the brotherhood which runs the church:

Confraternita dei Legnaioli

In 1817 the Brotherhood of Carpenters moved into the church and they are still their today. At Christmas the brotherhood displays its carpentry skills and produces beautiful wooden nativity scenes which are much enjoyed by the locals.

Walk to the other end of the Piazza.

Leave the square by the left hand street through an archway and along narrow Via del Gallo. This will take you to a crossroads with Via del Battistero where you turn right.

Via del Battistero

This street is the centre of Lucca's antiques market. In fact there is an antiques market in Lucca on the third Sunday of every month, so you might see it in action depending on when you visit. If the market is not on, you can still window-shop in the many little antique shops which line this street.

Continue along this road to walk into Piazza San Giusto on your right.

Piazza San Giusto

It's a pretty square so you might like to stop for refreshment as you are just about at the end of this walk. It's a shame that Caffe Pucci, Lucca's first coffee shop from 1700, is no longer here.

If you remember the Potted History, the Lombards brought their financial skills to Lucca. This square was the original home of Lucca's mint which was opened by the Lombards in the seventh century. Coins were minted here until the eleventh century when the mint was moved to another part of the city. Lucca was still minting coins until 1843.

There is a large arts and crafts market here every last weekend of the month.

San Giusto

Take a look at the little church sitting on the square with its two lions guarding the ornate doorway. The church dates from about the eleventh century. Look carefully behind the lions and you will see two faces staring back out at you. In fact the whole façade is really quite ornate once you look at it carefully, with lilies, leaves, and fantastical animals carved into the stonework.

Face way from the church and cross the square diagonally right.

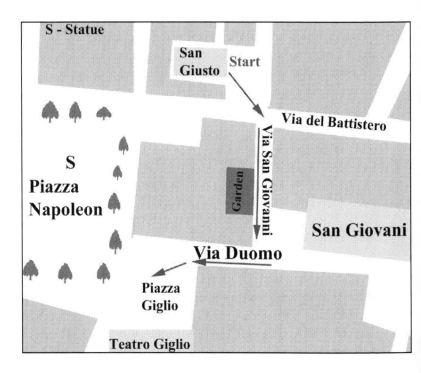

With the church door behind you, cross the square diagonally right. Leave the square by little Via San Giovanni. You will pass a walled garden on your right and then reach a square which you should recognise as you walked through it at the start of this walk.

Turn right to return to Piazza Giglio where this walk started.

Walk 2 – Lucca West

This walk starts in Piazza Napoleone.

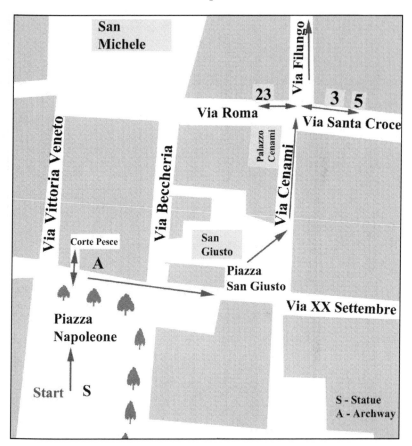

Piazza Napoleone

This large square is known as Piazza Grande to the locals. It has been the political heart of Lucca since Castruccio Castracani built his Augusta Fortress on this spot when he was elected ruler of Lucca, having defeated and expelled Pisa which was ruling Lucca at the time. The Augusta Fortress was an enormous building and actually covered about a quarter of Lucca at that time.

When the popular Castracani died, his young sons did not have the ability to hold onto power, so the family was exiled and other ambitious families took control. The rulers that followed Castracani were much more interested in personal gain than Lucca's fortune, and eventually turned into tyrants. Lucca revolted, killed the tyrants, and the by then hated fortress was burned to the ground.

The square you see today is much more French than Italian. The square was rebuilt by Elisa Bonaparte, Napoleon's sister, who was a popular ruler. A statue of Napoleon was planned for the square, but as we know Napoleon's reign came to a sudden end at Waterloo, and instead you see Duchesse Marie Louise of Spain, who took over from the Napoleon family.

The square is ringed by lovely plane trees which provide welcome shade from Italy's hot summers. The cars moved in during the twentieth century, but were evicted in 1998, and now the square is a lovely place to sit or explore.

Stand face to face with Marie Louise and behind you is the Ducal Palace

Palazzo Ducale

Castracani's fortress also covered the ground the palace now stands on. Once the fortress was burned down in the fourteenth century, this palace was built to replace it and is where Lucca has been governed from since then. It has been redesigned a few times. Don't worry about exploring it right now as you will walk through the palace at the end of this walk.

Stand face to face with Marie Louise once again and turn left. Walk down to the end of the square. You will see an archway in front of you and a small street on its left.

Corte del Pesce

If you would like a peep at a really old part of Lucca, take a few steps into the little street, not the archway. You will enter a medieval courtyard which was where an old fish market used to be – from as far back as 1200 AD.

Lucca's market courtyards were generally run by a single family who lived in a tower house in the court. By day everyone was welcome for business, but at night the courtyard's entrances were closed to outsiders.

In fact there are several corte (courtyards) in Lucca which were dedicated to selling a single item. Sadly at the time of writing, this one is rather neglected and could so easily be restored.

Return to Piazza Napoleone and turn left to go along Via XX Settembre. Pass Via Beccheria on your left and you will enter a smaller square with some flowers and statue of an angel holding up a laurel wreath.

Monument to the Fallen

It is by Urbano Lucchesi who also sculpted the statue of Garibaldi which you saw at the start of Walk 1. It is dedicated to those who died in defence of Italy and the inscription says:

Ai Caduti per la Patria

which translates as:

The Fallen for the Homeland

Continue straight ahead to reach Piazza San Giusto on your left. Cross the square diagonally to reach Via Cenami. Go along Via Cenami and you will see Palazzo Cenami on your left at the end of the street.

Palazzo Cenami

The palace was built for the Arnolfini family by Nicolao Civitali, the son of Lucca's famous architect Matteo Civitali whose work you've already seen. The palazzo was sold seventy years later to the Cenami family.

The palazzo is lined with stone benches, and this has always been a very popular place for the locals to sit and chat, and for tourists to take a breather.

When you reach the end of the palazzo you will be on Via Santa Croce. Turn right along Santa Croce just a few steps to number 3.

Giovanni Sercambi

You will see a plaque which commemorates the work of Giovanni Sercambi – an author from Lucca who lived in the fourteenth century. He wrote "The Chronicles of Lucca", a ongoing history of Lucca, until he died of the plague in 1424, and his books added a lot to our knowledge of Lucca's past.

Take another few steps to reach number 5.

Manifatture

This is a lovely Art Nouveau façade with the word Manifaturre flanked by two intriguing faces. It must have been a factory of some sort long ago. At the time of writing it's a fashionable opticians.

Return to the junction and walk a little beyond to reach Via Roma 23.

Galliano

Here is another lovely Art Nouveau shop façade, the premises of Ditta Galliani. This is a shop for luxury items and its fitting it should have an imposing façade, with the marble bust sitting above the name of the store.

The sign tells us it was founded in 1819. The Galliani family no longer owns the business but the new owners have kept the lovely façade and have restored the interior.

Return to the junction once more and this time and turn left into Via Fillungo.

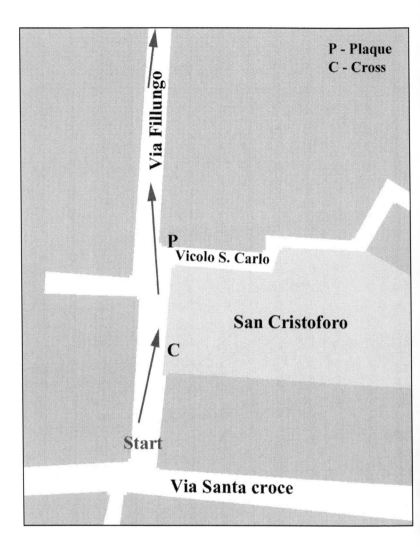

You will find San Cristoforo on your right.

San Cristoforo

This church was first mentioned in 1053. The architect designed it in the style loved by Pisa, with columns at the front topped with arches.

At one time there was an iron cross embedded in the façade on the right hand side of the main door. The cross was made of two iron measures which were used to measure cloth by the weaver's guild, to ensure there was no swindling going on. At the time of writing the cross has been removed although you can still see the outline of where it sat. Perhaps they will restore it some day in the future.

This church has been "restored" and "improved" several times over the centuries, the last time in 1940 when the plaster was removed and the fittings were stripped. It became a memorial to Lucca's war dead when their names were carved onto the walls. It is now deconsecrated and you will probably find an exhibition in place. It is worth going in if it's open, as it is a poignant memorial.

Matteo Civitali

When you exit the church, spot the plaque on the wall of Vicolo San Carlo on your right. It commemorates Matteo Civitali who lived there.

Continue along Via Fillungo.

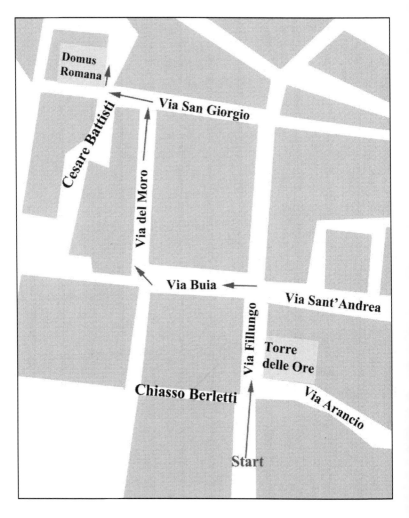

Pause for a moment when you reach Chiasso Barletti on your left.

Chiasso Berletti

It was on the corner of Chiasso Berletti and Via Fillungo that Caesar, Pompey, and Crassus met in 55 BC. They met to reform their political alliance which was called the First Triumvirate – and they basically agreed who would rule which parts of the Roman Empire for the next five years. A very historic spot!

Continue a few steps along Via Filungo to reach the Torre delle Ore entrance.

Torre delle Ore

It's a very old tower and the highest in the city. It was built at the end of the fourteenth century. If you have the energy you can purchase a ticket to climb the 207 wooden steps to the top.

You will get a great view of the city and its surroundings, as well as being able to get a close up view of the clockwork mechanism and bells.

When you exit the tower turn right to reach the crossroads with Via Sant'Andrea and Via Buia. You already passed this point on Walk One. This time turn left into Via Buia, and then turn right into Via del Moro.

When you reach the T junction turn left along Via San Giorgio. At the next corner turn right into via Cesare Batistti and on your left you will see the Domus Romana – with its very ornate stone entrance.

Domus Romana

Lucca has an interesting law which came into being in 2000. If anyone wants to dig deeper than 30cm they have to have a site survey done first. Why? Because below Lucca lies the old Roman city, and Lucca is very keen to save any parts of it which come to light. It's very good for the tourism business.

The owners of this house planned a wine cellar in 2010, and as luck would have it the diggers found some Roman relics, including old Roman walls, coins with Tiberius's head, and a sculpted gorgon's head flanked by two boys riding on dolphins.

The owner scrapped the wine cellar and instead we have this little museum. If you choose to go in, you descend below street level and will first be shown a short film with English subtitles about Roman Lucca. It shows what the archaeologists think the house looked like in Roman times, but it has to be said that not much of it remains today.

After the film you can look around the excavations, or take up the offer of a guided tour from the attendant. There are two rooms showing the excavated Roman stone work and artefacts.

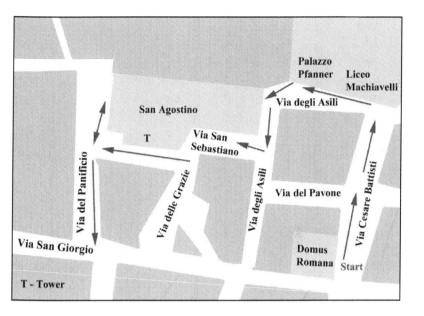

From the museum door, turn left to continue up Via Cesare Battisti. Pass via Del Pavone on your left and take the next left Via Degli Asilli.

As you turn into Via Degli Asilli you will see the Liceo classico Niccolò Machiavelli on your right.

Liceo classico Niccolò Machiavelli

It's the oldest school in Lucca and one of the oldest in Italy.

Lucca started educating its citizens in the early nineteenth century, and this building soon grew to be a university with law, medicine and surgery faculties. Later however Lucca was swept up into the Grand Duchy of Tuscany and ruled from Florence, and as a consequence it lost the right to have a university. The university was demoted to a school and it remains a school today.

It has kept some of its treasures from its university days, such as its huge naturalist collection, its scientific instruments collection, and even two mummies brought from Thebes in Egypt in 1820. At the time of writing there are talks about opening its museum to visitors, so maybe by the time you visit you will be able to venture in.

Continue along Via Degli Asilli. On your right you will find the entrance to the Palazzo Pfanner.

Palazzo Pfanner

This is a beautiful palace in a pretty garden – a rare splash of greenery in Lucca. So buy a ticket and pop in.

The Palazzo is still owned by the Pfanner family who are gradually restoring the palace and opening more of it to sightseers. It featured as a setting in Jane Campion's movie "The Portrait of a Lady".

The palace was acquired by Felix Pfanner in the early nineteenth century. Felix was a brewer from Austria. He was invited by Charles Louis Bourbon, the Duke of Lucca, to teach the Italians how to brew beer. He opened his brewery in the cellar of this palazzo in1846 and progressively acquired the entire building. His brewery was the first in the Duchy of Lucca and one of the first in Italy. The brewery and its beer garden were situated between the garden and the cellars of the Palazzo but it closed in 1929.

You should definitely visit the garden with its lawns, fountain, flower gardens, and pots of lemon trees, dotted with statues of the Greek Gods and the figures of the four elements, Volcano (Fire), Mercury (Air), Dionysus (Earth), and Ocean (Water).

If you also opt to visit the palace, go up the grand staircase to the main reception room which is bright with frescos. You will find a museum of the silk and costumes worn in Lucca in the seventeenth and eighteenth centuries.

If you take the bike ride around the wall you can look right down into the garden, but it's not quite the same as sitting in it, and enjoying the fragrance of lemons and the sound of tinkling water.

Leave the garden and turn right into Via degli Asili and follow it round the corner. Take the first right, Via San Sebastiano, and you will find you are walking along the side of a church, Sant'Agostino. It zig-zags a few times before you reach the front.

Sant'Agostino

You will notice that the bell tower is built on a very old wall which is actually part of Lucca's old Roman Theatre.

Continue to the front of the church and go in if it's open – it has an interesting story.

The church has three chapels and one of them contains the image of the Madonna Del Sasso, which means Madonna of the Stone. Legend tells us that a gambler asked the Madonna for help in a bet, lost the bet, and decided to throw a stone at this image. The Madonna began to bleed and a pit opened up sending the gambler to hell.

There is actually a mark on the Madonna's shoulder, and even spookier there is a trapdoor below the painting marked by the words:

> Injuring and making the Virgin bleed
> The impious man fell endlessly
> Be merciful!

The legend also tells us that before the trapdoor was installed, the congregation would occasionally lower a dog into it, and then pull it out again to find it a bit charred – as proof it was a gate to hell.

Leave the church and turn left along Piazza Sant'Agostino to reach a T junction with Via San Giorgio.

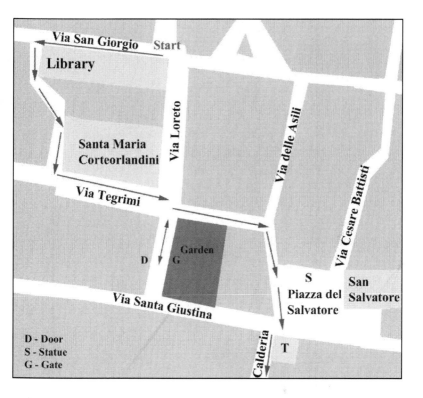

Turn right into Via San Giorgio and then take the first left along Via Santa Maria Corteorlandini. It will wiggle left and open out and you will see Lucca's state library on your left.

Biblioteca Statale di Lucca

This is regarded as one of the most beautiful libraries in Italy. It sits in the old convent of the church which you will be visiting shortly, Santa Maria Corteorlandini.

Its collection includes rare and ancient books which sit in the beautiful baroque library room at the top. Sadly that room is not open to the public except on special open days - tours can be requested but for now they are in Italian only.

Continue along Via Santa Maria Corteorlandini to reach the front of the church.

Santa Maria Corteorlandini

This church is often missed by tourists as it is a bit off the tourist trail but it is well worth a look inside. At one time it was one of the most important in the city and it's beautifully decorated inside to match its status.

The church has another unofficial name, "Santa Maria Nera". It gets that name because inside there is a very much simpler chapel which is accessed by a door on the left hand side of the nave. It is a replica of part of the Holy House of Loreto in Italy, where a wooden Madonna with a black face is worshipped.

The Holy House of Loreto was apparently where The Annunciation took place – the Virgin Mary was given the glad tidings by the archangel Gabriel. In the twelfth century Turkey was invading Nazareth and according to legend a band of angels uprooted the house and carried it to Loreto in Italy for safety.

This replica includes one brick which according to legend came from the original Holy House – although there is no indication of which brick it might be.

When you leave the church, turn left to go around it along Piazza San Giovanni Leonardi. You will reach a side door into the church, topped with the usual two lions.

In 2017 an archaeological dig by the church door uncovered six medieval graves, but sadly mindless vandals destroyed the remains found in two of the graves.

Walk into Via Tegrimi to reach a junction with Via Loreto.

Turn right into Via Loreto, and if you are lucky you will find the gate to the walled garden on your left open. If it is you can step in to sit under a tree for a little rest, and even if it's locked you can peep through the wall windows to see it. Also take a look at the very impressive doorway opposite the garden entrance.

When you are ready return to the junction and turn right to continue on Via Tegrimi - you can get another look at the garden through the wall windows as you do. Finally turn right onto Via delle Asili to reach Piazza del Salvatore.

Piazza del Salvatore

This square has been rescued from the dreaded car, and is now a nice place to explore and relax.

The square has a nickname, Pupporona, which means Large Breasts. It earned that name when the lovely statue on the fountain was installed. The lady is a Naiad and she is wearing a robe rather loosely draped around her. When it was first unveiled, conservative Lucca was outraged at the nudity. The bishop demanded its removal but it survived.

By the way the water from the taps is from the mountains and is clear and fresh and the locals often make use of it. So if you are carrying a water bottle you could top it up. Don't miss having a look at the fountain's massive lion paws!

The yellow building behind the fountain was at one time the home of Boccherini, Lucca's other musical son who you saw a statue of on Walk One.

Opposite the fountain is an old medieval tower which you can see only has little holes for windows. This was a defence tower and there was no external access – the only way in was via the adjoining building. It's thought that the stones you see jutting out would have supported a temporary wooden stairway, which could be easily dismantled if under attack.

San Salvatore

If you stand face to face with Pupporona, the church of San Salvatore stands on your right-hand side – It's a very old church, dating from the twelfth century. A large crack appeared in the church when Lucca's water table moved, but it has been restored and the church is safe once more.

Above the right-hand door is a carving showing us one of the miracles of Saint Nicholas. The left-hand side shows Adeodata, a young man who was captured and enslaved by the Saracens – he is shown serving at the table of the Emir. His mother prayed to Saint Nicholas, so in the middle we see Saint Nicholas grabbing Adeodata by the hair and taking him home. Finally on the right Adeodata is safely home, and is serving at the priest's table.

Before leaving the square walk round the church to find its fourth door. Above the door is another carving showing Nicholas being baptised. Even the little columns on either side of Saint Nicholas are beautifully carved with spirals running up them. The font has the sculptors name engraved on it – Biduino who came from Pisa.

Leave the square by the road on one side of the old medieval tower, Via Calderia,

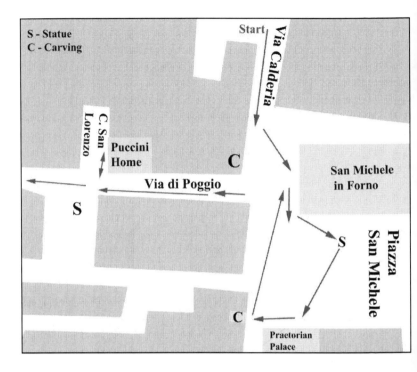

You will reach Piazza San Michele and its church San Michele in Foro. Piazza San Michele is where Lucca declared independence from Pisa in 1369.

Francesco Burlamacchi

Standing outside the church is Francesco Burlamacchi – not a name you might recognize. He was a revolutionary who wanted the free cities of Tuscany to form a republic quite independent from the all-powerful Medici family and Florence. He was betrayed, tortured, and executed for his views, and it took until the nineteenth century for Lucca to erect a memorial to his worthwhile opinions.

Chiesa di San Michele in w

As you now know Lucca has a Roman history, and the name of this church celebrates the spot where the Roman Forum once stood. This square is where Lucca was governed during the Roman Empire. In fact the seat of government stayed right here, long after the Romans had gone. Centuries later it was transferred to Piazza Napoleone as the Augusta Fortress.

The first church was built here in the eighth century, and it lay on part of the Francigena, the pilgrim's route to Rome. The pilgrims would make their way through the narrow lanes of Lucca and arrive in this open piazza to rest and pray.

The pilgrims would use a wooden bridge to cross a little stream, the Fossa Natali, which crossed the square. Recent excavations using the latest technology to scan the ground have located the path it took.

The present day church was built on top of the original church by order of Pope Alexander II in the 11th century. If you walk to the right hand side of the church and stand back, you can see that the façade is much higher than the church body. Why? They simply ran out of money.

It was constructed of limestone, and it's topped with an impressive statue of the archangel Michael slaying a dragon. Urban legend tells us that the Archangel wears an emerald and when the sun hits it at the right angle, it sparkles for all to see. No-one has ever found the emerald – although there have been reports of sighting the green sparkle. It would be nice if it was true.

The bell tower was originally higher. When Pisa gained control of Lucca in the fourteenth century, the Doge of Pisa ordered that it be shortened as it was taller than the tallest tower in Pisa.

Stand back and look up above the columns. You will see black and white marble inlays which depict all sorts of animals fighting with other animals. It's quite difficult to see but there are also heads at the top of some of the columns. They were placed there during a restoration in the nineteenth century, so they are of famous personalities of the time, like Garibaldi.

At one time there was a marble Madonna and Child by Civitali on the right hand corner of the façade. It was put there in gratitude for the end of the terrible Black Death in 1476. However like other churches, the original has been put inside for safety, and replaced with a copy to withstand the Italian weather.

The church has an impressive entrance with seven arches topping five ornate Corinthian columns. The lintel above the main entrance is decorated with a frieze of mythical animals, and a tiny Saint Michael killing a dragon with a lance. Above that are two rather sad looking lions.

Now go inside the church to explore.

Find Filippino Lippi's 1479 painting of Saint Helen, Saint Jerome, Saint Sebastian and Saint Roch - it's on the right-hand side of the altar. All the saints are wearing bright eye-catching robes which draw your eyes to look at it.

Saint Roch stands on the left. He survived the plague and he is always depicted showing a nasty sore. Saint Jerome stands next to Saint Helen, with a lion peeping from behind his robe – he removed a thorn from a lion's paw in the desert. Do look at the beautifully transparent veils draped around Saint Helen.

You can also find the sculpture Madonna and Child which was brought indoors for safety, and replaced with a copy outside. It's near the main door.

When you are ready to move on, exit the church.

Praetorian Palace

Stand with your back to the church door and turn left to see the beautiful palace with its four archways and topped by a lovely clock. It used to be the mayor's office but is now the court. Take a walk over for a look.

The archway area is often used for exhibitions; you never know what you might come across when passing. The chap sitting in the chair in the middle of the loggia is Matthew Civitali – you have seen several of his works already on this walk. He was originally a barber but decided he could do better. He designed the Volto Santo temple you saw earlier and was also the designer of the Praetorian Palace itself. When he died, the building was completed by his son.

Face the palace and turn right.

The Volto Santo

Look up to between the first and second floor to see a carving of the Volto Santo, which you will recognise if you have already visited the Cathedral on Walk 1.

Return to the square and head back to the front of the church. Stand with your back to the church door, and walk straight ahead towards Via di Poggio.

Before you go down Via di Poggio take a look at the two chubby little sculpted figures at number 5, just to the right of the entrance to Via di Poggio.

Now walk into Via di Poggio.

Puccini family home

Continue to reach Piazza Cittadella on your left where a bronze Puccini sits. Stand face to face with Puccini, and behind him lies little Corte San Lorenzo, where you will find the entrance to the Puccini family home.

Puccini was born in Lucca and this is the family home where he and his six siblings were raised. His great-great grandfather was the first great musician in the family, followed by his great grandfather, his grandfather, his father, and finally the star of the family Giacomo Puccini. The family held the post of Maestro di Cappella (Choirmaster) in Lucca for 124 years, and the line was only broken because Puccini's father died when Giacomo was only six – a bit too young even for a genius!

His family however made sure that the musical dynasty survived this break, Giacomo studied music in Lucca and finally Milan. He went on to compose many operas, the most famous being Madame Butterfly, La Boheme, and Tosca – although his best works were all written when he lived elsewhere.

Inside the house you can see the Steinway piano which he practiced on and which he used to compose Turandot, his unfinished opera.

Puccini obviously loved music, but he was also an engineer and invented the first off-road vehicle. He was also one of the first drivers to be granted a license in Italy. Sadly Puccini also loved to smoke and came to an unpleasant end, dying of throat cancer.

Gelateria Santini

If you fancy an ice-cream you could do worse than try Gelateria Santini. Stand facing the same way as Puccini and cross the square diagonally right to find it. It opened its doors in 1916 and has been in the same family since then – although now they use modern equipment to make it.

Return to the Puccini statue once more, stand face to face with Puccini, and turn left to leave the square on via di Poggio.

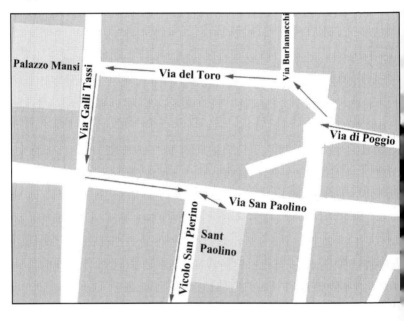

You will reach a very irregular square, so keep to the right hand side. Pass Via Burlamacchi on the right and leave the square by Via del Toro. Follow this straight road to reach the Palazzo Mansi.

Palazzo Mansi

This was the Mansi family home, a 17th century palace. The family home is now a museum but is worth a visit in its own right. It celebrates the wealth and success of the Mansi family. The palace was purchased by the Italian State in 1966, restored and filled with Luchesse art and furnishings, as the originals had mostly been lost. However the original decorations are still in place and are quite eye-catching.

I am sure you remember the story of Lucida Mansi from the Botanical Garden visit. Another version of Lucida's story tells us that when the devil came to claim his prize, he dragged her down to hell through a pit which appeared in a bedroom of the Palace. Legend says that the pit could not be filled in and it was finally closed by a circular cover.

Yet another story tells us that the hole was a murderous trap where Lucida dispatched lovers she was tired of, to ensure they couldn't sully her reputation. From the tales told about her it doesn't sound as though she was very successful.

Actually poor Lucida had a sad enough fate without being snatched by the devil. She was a widow at 22 and it's thought that she died of the plague in 1649. Her family tried to forget about her, destroyed paintings of her, and burned any legal documents relating to her. The location of her grave is unknown.

When you enter the palace you will be greeted by an impressive coach, and you can imagine Lucida gadding about town looking for her next lover.

Once upstairs on the first floor, turn left to visit the formal apartments first. The rooms are sumptuously decorated, have beautiful chandeliers, and there are colourful frescoes everywhere. You will eventually reach the smaller family rooms, which are still worth a quick whizz round. You can try to imagine which one was Lucida's.

The Music Room

This room was decorated to celebrate a family wedding, and you can still see the wooden balcony where the orchestra would have led the festivities.

Some of the colourful frescoes tell the story of Emperor Aurelianus and Zenobia, Queen of Palmyra.

She was said to be even more beautiful than Cleopatra, highly educated, but also loved to hunt. She expanded her empire which eventually stretched from Egypt to modern day Turkey. However Emperor Aurelianus brought his army east to meet the Palmyrian army at Antioch, and the Roman army proved the stronger. Zenobia was taken prisoner to Rome. There are two endings to the story, the sad one has her beheaded, the happier one has her given a villa in Italy where she married and had a family.

The Alcove Room

This is a stunning room with carved and golden wood, frescoes, and sumptuous fabrics. Especially lovely are the caryatids, pillars in female form, which stand at the entrance to the alcove itself.

The ceiling shows us the story of Cupid and Psyche, one of the Greek myths. Psyche is a beautiful princess, so beautiful that even the god Cupid falls in love with her. His mother Venus sets Psyche impossible tasks which she must perform if she wishes to be united with Cupid. Love is never easy in Greek mythology.

Paintings

The museum does not have any really famous paintings, but the galleries are worth a stroll around. The palace's own original art collection was pinched by Charles Louis of Bourbon when the French ruled Lucca. So these paintings were given to Lucca as a replacement.

There is a small gallery on the first floor which you access from a corner of the Music Room. There are further galleries upstairs on the second floor.

Below are some favourites. Annoyingly they sometimes only open up the first floor of the Palazzo. So although you will see all the state chambers and apartments mentioned, you may not find all the paintings mentioned below if the second floor is closed. However you might be lucky.

Portrait of Pompey Guasparini dressed in summer - Antonio Franchi

This painting is by Antonio Franchi who came from Lucca and was nicknamed Il Lucchese. He trained here in Lucca before moving to the hub of art, Florence, where he became a favourite of the wealthy Florentine families. He died in Florence.

Here he has painted Pompeo Guasparini, one of Lucca's wealthy silk merchants, draped in expensive robes and holding ears of wheat which is said to symbolise summer.

Portrait of a Youth in a Pink Cloak– Pontormo

This is an unusual painting just because the emphasis is on the very pink outfit rather than the subject. It's thought the young man was a member of the powerful Medici family from Florence.

Strage degli Innocenti - Edoardo Gelli

This is just such a sad painting. It shows the death of a baby and his grieving mother after Herod's soldiers have murdered the new-born boys in Jerusalem.

L'incontro - Luigi De Servi

In complete contrast, this is such a happy picture, the lady portrayed is full of life and even her dog seems full of the joys.   Luigi De Servi came from Lucca. He travelled to Buenos Aires to make his fortune, and then returned to his beloved Lucca and opened his own studio there.

Puccini - Luigi De Servi

This is by the same artist as L'incontro.   It's only fitting that there should be a portrait of Puccini in Lucca.

When you leave the museum, turn right into Via Galli Tassi, which will take you to a junction with Via San Paolino. Turn left, and not far along you will reach the church of San Paolino on your right at the top of a little set of steps - very handy if you need to sit down for a few minutes.

San Paolino

The street and church are named after Lucca's first bishop who was a disciple of Saint Peter.   He was dispatched to Lucca to convert the locals and he was very successful, so he then tried to convert the rest of Tuscany including Pisa.   His luck ran out and he and several disciples were murdered in AD 69 on the border between Lucca and Pisa, supposedly on the order of Nero. History tells us that his remains were buried in a church near where he was murdered.

Roll on to 1261 when a monk from Lucca, Fra Jacopo, had a dream where he was told to visit the church of Sant'Antonio and attend mass. During the mass a voice whispered in his ear, telling him that the remains of San Paolino were buried beneath were he stood. The stones were torn up and as the sun set the diggers found a burial, containing the remains of not just Paolino but other priests who were killed at the same time. The remains of San Paolino were transferred to Lucca and placed in this church.

In 1662 Lucca fired a cannon to honour their Saint, but by mistake it was aimed at a crowd of pilgrims entering the city. To everyone's horror the cannonball hit the visitors but amazingly no one was injured, so this was instantly declared a miracle. Every twelfth of July, Lucca marks the occasion with The Feast of Saint Paolino. During the day there is a costumed crossbow competition and cannon-firing, and at night there is a torch lit procession.

There is a statue of San Paolino on one side of the main door – and on the other is San Donato, whose church was demolished just before this one was built.

If the church is open do pop in, as it has lots of colourful frescoes. Near the entrance are two fonts carved in marble by Matteo Civitali.

Find the Chapel of the Virgin which has an interesting painting of "The Coronation of the Virgin" with Lucca and its mighty wall at the bottom. Also you can find the chapel which houses the sarcophagus with the remains of San Paolino.

Puccini was an organist in this church at the start of his musical career.

When you exit the church turn left and left again down Vicolo San Pierino.

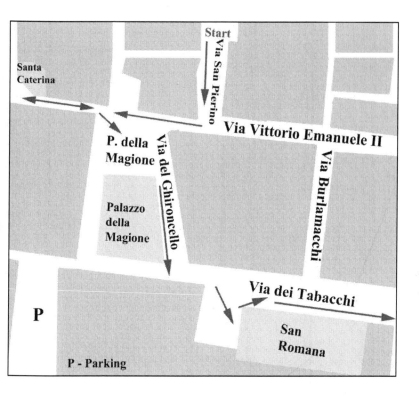

This little street will open out into Piazza san Pierino. Just walk straight ahead crossing the piazza and into via San Pierino.

You will reach one of the main roads in Lucca, Via Vittorio Emanuele II. Turn right for a short distance to reach a square on your left – it is usually full of cars. Keep walking along Via Vittorio Emanuele II to the next corner where you will find the Santa Caterina church on your right.

Santa Caterina

You will immediately spot that it's very unusual, as it was built to fit onto a rounded corner. For a long time it lay

101

neglected and was near collapsing, but it was saved and restored by IFA, the Italian Environment Fund who are dedicated to maintaining Italy's heritage. The church was restored, and finally reopened in 2014.

It stands in front of what was a tobacco factory and was where the factory workers prayed – so it got the nickname of The Church of the Cigar Makers.

It is well worth a visit. Inside you will find an oval church decorated with extravagant exuberance. The ladies on either side of the altar are Charity and Purity.

Stand under the dome and look up to see Santa Caterina surrounded by flying angels, and of course San Paolino who you have just been reading about. You are actually looking up through the dome oculus at a fresco stuck on the roof. It gives the appearance of a painting suspended high above you. You can climb a spiral staircase to reach the roof and see how it's put together – much less pretty but interesting.

When you leave, turn left to return back along Via Vittorio Emanuele II and cross over to Piazza della Magione.

Palazzo della Magione

Ignore the cars and instead have a look at the building with a balcony behind the bust of Carlo Angeloni. He was a tutor of Puccini - he also wrote operas but never achieved the fame of his pupil.

The building behind Carlo is the Palazzo della Magione Temple and was where the Knights Templar headquarters stood alongside a church and hospital.

The Knights Templar was a charitable military organization closely linked to the Crusades, the campaigns by Christian Europe to free the Holy Land. The knights were extremely powerful for over two centuries while the Crusades were in operation. When they were eventually ousted, another organisation known as the Knights of Saint John of the Cross, whose home was in Malta and who were a more benign organization, took their place. Lucca however limited their power and influence as they were seen as yet another foreign power trying to gain control. When Lucca declared itself a republic the Knights of Malta were also asked to leave.

In 1637 the palace was renovated and it was discovered that its foundations partly consist of Lucca's oldest walls. The palace was revamped again in the nineteenth century and the many coats of arms which used to cover the building were stripped – a great pity.

Stand back to back with Carlo Angeloni and leave the square by Via del Ghironcello on the left side of the palazzo. You will walk alongside another walled garden on your right but it's usually closed.

Turn left into Via dei Tabacchi. The church like building on your right is actually the Museum of Comics. Continue along Via dei Tabacchi to reach a tree-filled square and you will find the entrance.

Museum of Comics

Lucca actually hosts an annual convention of Comics and Gaming, so if you happen to be in town that week you will be surrounded by Batman, Lara Croft, and every other comic/game character you can think of.

It started in 1965 and grew in size but due to lack of funds it died away and the participants visited other cities instead like Rome. However it was rebooted in 2006 and Lucca now hosts the largest comic convention in Europe.

So it's only fitting that Lucca has a museum dedicated to comics, although it's probably only of interest to comic aficionados. The building has been undergoing restoration but if you are keen, hopefully it will be complete and you can explore the exhibits

Opposite the museum is another old church.

San Romana

As mentioned in the potted history, the huge Augustus fortress which stood nearby was destroyed in the thirteenth century. So when the Dominican order started to build this church they simply recycled the bricks from the ruins. It looks unfinished on the outside because it never was - the bricks were supposed to be covered in marble but that turned out to be too expensive.

The church has been deconsecrated and the interior restored to turn it into a rather unique auditorium. That does mean unfortunately that it's usually closed to the public.

You can see some large tombs standing outside along the wall; they belonged to some of Lucca's wealthy merchant families.

Walk along the left side of the church on Via dei Tabacchi and take a look at the tombs as you do.

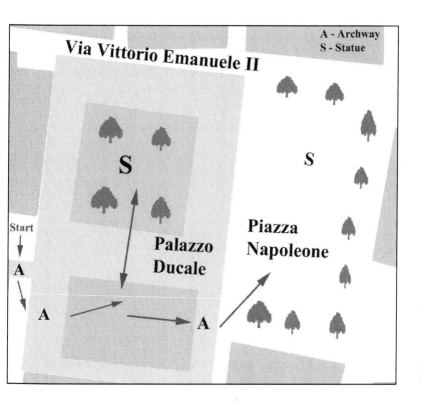

When you reach the end of the road, turn right through a huge archway. You will then see a smaller archway on your left which you can use as a shortcut to reach Lucca's main square. Go through it to enter a large internal courtyard.

Walk into the courtyard and then take one of the archways on your left to enter a second courtyard filled with trees.

Cortile Carrara

It is called Cortile Carrara, and is named after the chap whose statue sits in the middle. Francesco Carrara was a politician and lawmaker from the nineteenth century who campaigned for the end of the death penalty in Europe.

The square is surrounded by the Palazzo Ducale. It was built after the Augustus Fortress was destroyed and Lucca's rulers always lived there. These days it is where Lucca is governed from. The palace is not open to the public except on special open days.

Now retreat back to the first courtyard and turn left through another archway to return you to Piazza Napoleone and the end of the walk.

Walk 3 - The Wall

The enormous wall which surrounds Lucca was erected for defence in the 16th and 17th centuries. We owe the wall's survival to the fact that Lucca didn't really get involved in the Tuscan battles and wars once it was built, unlike Florence, Siena, and Pisa. The walls reach 12 metres high and the circuit is about 4km.

You can walk around, but the best option is to hire bikes from any of the hire shops – there is even one at the station. You might also find that your hotel will provide free bikes to guests.

You could also take some food and drinks with you as there are several nice spots to stop for a picnic. A personal favourite is the San Paolino bastion.

Once you are saddled up you should ride around the old town a couple of times. It doesn't take very long and gives a real idea of the size and character of the town. The wall is very wide, tree-lined, and perfectly safe. You can ride under the shady trees, stopping wherever you like to take a picture or just sit on a bench and enjoy the view.

As you go round, notice the four types of tree you pass under: Ilex, plane, chestnut, and lime. The trees were not actually put there for the walkers benefit, but to provide an anchor for the packed down soil used when the wall was constructed. It wasn't until the nineteenth century that the walls were declared a public walkway – and they have been used enthusiastically by Lucca ever since.

As you go round you will pass over many gates. Some are just holes in the wall, but some are interesting enough to cycle/walk down from the wall to have a look at.

The gates proved useful in 1812. They were sealed shut to help save Lucca from the flooding River Serchio which lies just outside the city.

This walk takes you around the wall and points out the sights as you go round. You can follow it from whichever access point you use to get up to the wall. It runs anti-clockwise so just before you start cycling/walking, face in towards Lucca and turn right.

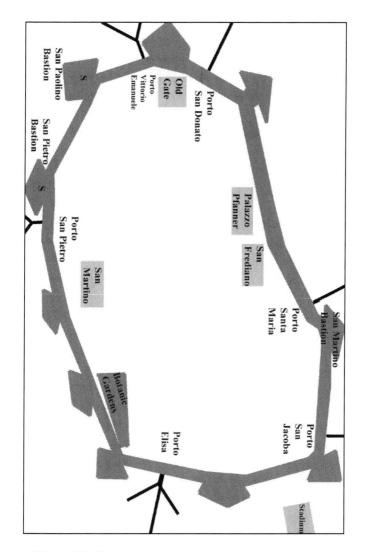

Porta Elisa – Wall access

This is the Eastern gate and here you will find both a ramp to get up on the wall, and a small gate to exit the city.

Lucca originally did not have a gate on the eastern side of the city for defence reasons. Florence lies to the east, so if the Florentine army attacked it would have to circle the city to find a way in. That would give Lucca more time to man the battlements.

This gate was only punched through the wall when Napoleon came to power. It was named after Napoleon's sister Elisa, who became the Grand Duchess of Tuscany. The gateway was made from the white marble of a demolished church.

As you cycle (or walk) to the next gate, look to your right to see the Stadio Porta Eliza, Lucca's football ground. Sadly their football team, Lucchese Libertas, is currently languishing in Lega Pro, Italy's third division league. It's an old team founded in 1905, and their greatest moment was in 1947 when they won Serie B, Italy's second division League.

Porta San Jacopo – Wall access

This northern gate is used mainly by cars and is one of the newest gates built in 1930. It is pretty characterless, just a hole in the wall.

Via del Fosso

Just a little further on stop again and face away from the city. Look down and you should be able to see a water channel entering the city – that is the source of the canal which runs along Via del Fosso which you will have crossed if you have already done Walk 1.

San Martino bastion

This fortification lies between the San Jacopo gate and the Santa Maria gate. The Wall is studded with bastions all round at regular intervals, and if Lucca had ever been attacked they would have provided a formidable defence.

From this bastion you get a good view of the Garfagnana, the mountains to the north.

Porta Santa Maria – Wall access

This is one of the original gates and it lies on the North side of the city. The city side gateway is very plain, so exit the city to see the much grander gateway on the other side. As hinted by its name it has a statue of the Madonna at the entrance, and two panther statues – the panther is the symbol of Lucca. One of the panthers is holding Lucca's coat of arms.

Return to the wall and continue your ride. A little further on you will get a very good view of the tower of San Frediano which lies very close to the wall.

Palazzo Pfanner Garden

Next up is the garden of Palazzo Pfanner which you visited on Walk Two.

Porta San Donato – Wall access a little way from the gate

The original San Donato gate was built in 1590 but only lasted fifty years. This second gate was then built to replace it. If you go outside the gate you can see the marble statues of San Paolino and San Donato.

The original San Donato gate still exists although it is no longer attached to the wall. If you are standing above the Porta San Donato, the old gate is over to your right.

Porta Vittorio Emanuele

This gate is the main city gate and where most of the traffic comes and goes. Its official name is Vittorio Emanuele, but unofficially Porta Sant'Anna, named after the church which lies outside the wall.

San Paolino bastion

This is a particularly nice spot for a picnic if you are so inclined. The statue you see in the middle of the green is a memorial to Alfredo Catalani, another of Lucca's musical sons. He wrote operas, and it's perhaps a bit unfortunate that one of them is called La Wally.

San Pietro Bastion

As you approach Port San Pietro Bastion you will pass a statue of King Emmanuel which stands in front of the Café Antica della Mura. This much-loved restaurant was created from an old barracks in the late nineteenth century by Charles Louis of Bourbon.

Don't miss the three-legged lampposts guarded by lions.

Porto San Pietro – Wall access

Just beyond the café is Lucca's southern gate. It is decorated on the outside with St Peter in the centre, lions on each side, and the word "libertas" above. This was the only gate foreigners could enter by, a sort of medieval passport control.

Lucchese freedom

Outside the gate you will see a grassy traffic island and behind that stands a bronze equestrian statue. At the time of writing it is being restored, but perhaps it will be visible when you visit.

The knight on his horse is holding a banner bearing the Lucca coat of arms, and represents Luchesse freedom. It was unveiled in 1930 in the presence of King Vittorio Emanuele, and it's rather sad that it has stood there for nearly a century behind a wooden fence and been forgotten about.

The Volto Santo

You might decide to venture down and go through the gate to get a closer look at the knight. If you do then when you return through the gate, pause and look up above the portcullised internal gateway. You will see another rendition of the Volto Santo.

Cattedrale di San Martino

From the wall you will get a very good view of the Cathedral – so take a snap

Botanic Gardens

As you pass the botanical gardens, you may recall the story of the Devil and Lucida riding around the walls on a fiery carriage.

Your next stop will be back at Porto Elisa.

Did you enjoy these walks?

I do hope you found these walks both fun and interesting, and I would love feedback. If you have any comments, either good or bad, please review this book.

Other Tuscan Gems

Why not visit Florence, Siena or Pisa while you are in Tuscany. They are just a train ride away from Lucca and full of interesting sights. You can find other Strolling Around books on Amazon.

Printed in Great Britain
by Amazon